How to Deal with Gaslighting Abuse

Use Emotional Intelligence to Stop Manipulators, Toxic People and Narcissists

By

Bob Scott

Copyright

Printed in the United States of America
© 2019 by Bob Scott

ZeroNever Publishing House

USA | UK | Canada

Other Books by The Same Author

- <u>How to Deal with Gaslighting: Recognize and Stop Hidden Psychological Manipulations and Abuse</u>

- <u>How to Deal with Emotional Immaturity: Cope with Emotionally Immature People in A Relationship, Work and Social Life</u>

- <u>How to Deal with Negative People: Protect Your Boundaries, Build Confidence, And Gain Respect</u>

- <u>Change Your Life:</u> How to Overcome Anxiety, Depression and Negative Thinking

- <u>Anxiety and Phobia Workbook:</u> How to Overcome Anxiety and Panic Attacks

- <u>How to Deal with Difficult People:</u> Control the Situation! Overcome Your Annoying and Frustrating Coworkers, Friends, Parents, or Classmates

Table of Contents

CHAPTER ONE:

Understanding Gaslighting and Relationship Abuse

From time immemorial, humans have used all sorts of subtle manipulations to achieve their aims. The keyword here is subtle. You surely don't want to be seen. You don't want to be caught in the act. To be seen means your power over your victim is broken. Operating from the shadows is the trademark of successful manipulators. Manipulation has worked so far in our history because most times, we humans have that innate desire to be led. There is always that ideology, cult figure, or even material things where we may want to derive our personal achievements. These people or things give us a sense of purpose and direction. We all love this feeling of seeing our lives count for something. And whatever figure or philosophy that points us in this direction, we will gladly follow. Intelligent manipulators have sensed this need in us and have taken the cue to provide and fill up this vacuum in humans.

Manipulation is as old as humanity itself. If biblical stories are anything to go by, the world is in its current shambolic state because a woman allowed herself to be manipulated by a serpent. It has been used by men of old to achieve personal glory and kowtow men to their whims and caprices.

Gaslighting is a term that became only popular recently. With a lot of goings-on with the Donald Trump presidency, the term has been exported to the political scene to mean a scenario whereby facts are distorted, the reality is cancelled, and nothing is distorted by our political elites to mean something. The term simply refers to a situation where someone manipulates you into doubting your very own memory and view of reality. In the gaslighting process, your perceptions and sense of happenings around you are called into question. It gets to a point whereby you begin to second-guess your every move and might even doubt the essence of your existence. Do I really exist? Are my perceptions playing tricks on me? These questions begin to flood your mind. When it gets to this point, you've become an object for control by your gaslighter and only a plaything in his hands. You've simply been gaslighted. "His" is used in the neutral state here, because both genders can become victims of the gaslighting effect.

The research traces the origin of this word to a play by Patrick Hamilton titled "Gaslight" in 1938. It was the 1940 and 1944 movie adaptation of this play that popularized the term. In the movie, the husband of the gaslighting victim tries repeatedly to distort his wife's sense of reality in order to continue his series of murders and criminal activities. He constantly tells her she is delusional, crazy and out of tune with reality when she complains of the strange happenings in their home. This he does so well that he succeeded in changing her perceptions of happenings around her.

Gaslighting, as a term, has found its way into clinical psychology and mainstream psychotherapy to mean a form of relationship manipulation. Many people are now aware of its effect and are talking about it. While the gaslighting effect can be found in other spheres of our daily life - at the office, in our schools, between parents and children and even between siblings, it is the one that occurs in romantic relationships that seems to be widely reported. Gaslighting is what it is - psychological abuse and should not be tolerated. Understanding this concept in a relationship, recognizing it, naming it and shutting it down before its powerful hands grip you, is the way to recovery. Refuse to acknowledge it for what it is - outright manipulation, will have its devastating fangs getting at you.

CHAPTER TWO:

How To Know You Are Being Gaslighted

When left to thrive in a relationship, gaslighting portends doom for its victims. It can affect their emotional, psychological, physical, and spiritual well-being. Spotting this malaise from the onset and shutting it down will minimize its adverse impacts in our lives in the long run. So, how do you know that you are being gaslighted? The following signs can provide a clue:

- **When You are Habitually Lied To:** In my college days, I had this very good friend of mine, Vicka. We were best of friends and held no secret from each other. We were always discussing our plans with each other, talking about our current relationships, the boys, fashion trends, and other such mundane things young girls talk about. Vicka was a pretty lady in her early twenties, very smart and easy-going. She was able to make friends with people easily and turned every social event into a chance to meet someone new. She was very extroverted and had this vivacious personality. She met this charming medical student in one of the campus parties she attended and was swept off her feet by his charm and gentle mien. I for one thought he meant well for her, as he exuded this "can't hurt a fly" personality. He was unusually quiet, very charming and soft-spoken. One of the reasons Vicka caught the love bug. A relationship soon commenced between them and it seemed a match made in heaven. There was a period of bliss between them, the calm before the storm. Then came the downward spiral. He was a serial cheat and a liar, who lied even in the smallest, unnecessary things. When confronted over his cheating habits, he would lie outrightly and turned the whole affair against Vicka. The evidence was there - the ladies stuff all over his apartment, his disappearance for weeks on end, the calls he had to hide before he could take, the number of ladies that flocked to his apartment, even the way and manner he flirted with close friends of Vicka. All these he dismissed with a wave of the hand. On his birthday, though out of town, she decided to pay him a surprise visit. He got angry about why she should arrive unannounced and wouldn't let her in. She forced her way in and could see a lady hurriedly leaving through the back door. This he blatantly denied also. And was actually pretty angry she could even suggest she saw a lady in his apartment. He questioned the quality of her eyesight (she was actually shortsighted and wore glasses). He called her delusional and accused her of seeing things that were not there. Was her mind playing tricks on her? "Maybe I really didn't see a lady in there". She told herself "maybe the make-up kits in his bathroom are his sister's", even when she knew he got no female siblings. She repeatedly questioned her sanity. She made excuses for his many failings and tried to reconcile his lies with her own perceptions.

That, right there is the gaslighting effect in action. Gaslighters, when caught even red-handed, would look you right in the eye and tell you nothing of such occurred. You begin to question your own sense of reality - "is my mind playing tricks on me?". Gaslighters wants you to believe only their own version of events. Everything you say does not matter, only theirs does. They are habitual liars, who would over time come to believe their own lies. When with a gaslighting partner, refuse to believe their own version of events when all facts they put out points to the contrary.

- **When You Start Withholding Information From Friends And Family:** Vicka was one person who had never withheld information from me in the past. We knew each other's secret. We knew what was going on in each other's life at every given time. This was also extended to our different families, as our parents sometimes called either of us to get a clue on what the other party would like as a present on any memorable occasion. The bond was that strong. Not until Mr Charming came into the picture. Vicka wouldn't let me on whatever was happening in her life anymore. I lost count of the many times I had to lie to her family just to get her off some really tight situation. I was now the outsider. Mr Charming became the new go-to person for every kind of need. Evidently, my bestie was a victim of the gaslighting effect. She withheld information from me and her family members, so she wouldn't have to explain off certain things going wrong in her relationship.

- **They Compare You To Others:** Gradually he began to compare her to his past girlfriends. He once told her point blank that she was fat and would have to lose weight rapidly or he would look elsewhere. This was someone that had previously chided her on how skinny she looked. She religiously took to regimented eating and work-out programs. Fortunately, her discipline paid off and she lost some weight. She now had this killer figure most ladies could kill for. Yet, Mr Charming wasn't satisfied. She was left confused and in a state of hysteria. Where was this coming from? Why the sudden change of heart? This is the gaslighter's stock-in-trade. It is a control tool for them. Thus, with a gaslighter, you can never win their outright approval. For them, perfection is unattainable, and no matter how hard you try to meet their expectations, you will always fall short. So don't try to, to begin with.

- **You Constantly second-guess Yourself:** When it gets to that point where you now have to think through your every move or evaluate past decisions on the basis of whether he would like it or not, then you are neck-deep in the gaslighting effect. Being the lively and chatty type, Vicka would always want to engage and talk with people she just met. This usually gets Mr Charming pretty upset and he would accuse her of flirting with every guy she meets and rubbing it in his face. To win his much-needed approval, she retreated into her shell and stopped being that life-of-the-party she was.

  And that's the horror victims of gaslighting undergoes. They lose their identity. They lose themselves trying to bend to the will of their gaslighters. Instead of seeing him for who he was - The jealous, insecure boyfriend, she makes excuses for his behaviour. "I'm truly flirting with guys I just met and would have to stop". He twisted every innocent action of hers into something meant to hurt him. "You allowed that friend of yours take you to lunch. Don't you see how you're hurting my feelings?". She was trapped. A simple explanation will not do. She now has to evaluate every move before she makes them. In the guise of just being careful.

- **You Have A Sense Of Becoming A Totally Different Person:** You now have this constant feeling of being a different person. You know this is just not you. You're now someone else with a totally new world-view. What changed? You can't place your fingers on it. You just know you weren't like this.

- **When Friends Try Saving You From Yourself:** You friends have noticed the rapid changes in you. You just can't see it clearly yourself. Now they begin the quest of trying to save you from yourself. Their entreaties may meet brick wall though.

- **You Feel As Though You Can't Do Anything Right:** Your self-esteem has been eroded. This is what constant criticism from those you love causes. You're always trying to please him and failing constantly at it. The harder you try, the more unattainable it seems. So, you conclude, you can't do anything right anymore.

- **They Isolate You:** Gaslighters tend to isolate their victims from all who mean well for them - friends and family alike. "They are a bad influence for you" he repeats. The more this happens, the more you fall under their control. With friends and families left out in the cold, there's really no one watching out for you anymore.

- **It Is A One-sided Loyalty:** You can't count the number of times you've put your interest and maybe life down on the line for him. And what has he done for you? Nothing. Gaslighters expect fierce loyalty from their victims but are not ready to give one. Don't attempt to betray them. They would make you wish you hadn't. For them, it is loyalty or nothing. That, in itself, is not bad. Only that it is one-sided.

The list is endless and inexhaustible. Further research will provide you with more signs to look out for. The core fact to take out from your gaslighting abuse is that your sense of reality has been severely distorted. If you feel this signs read true, and your partner is gaslighting you, undermining your memories, perceptions and realities happening around you, then there's every chance you're a victim and should seek help.

CHAPTER THREE:

How To Spot A Gaslighter

- **They Never Apologise:** They never apologise. And when they eventually do, it is part of a plot to get something out of you. Dig deeper into their apologies and you may find out it wasn't really an apology, just one of their manipulative schemes to get you neck-deep in their control strategy.

- **They Lie Too Often:** It gets too often that it may become nerve-wracking for the victims. Why won't he just admit to the truth, even for once? You keep asking yourself. They lie about things that are not necessary. They are so caught up in the web of their own lies, that they tend to believe these lies themselves. This is a way of making everybody else see things through their own lenses.

- **They Use Your Weaknesses Against You:** In the initial stages of the relationship, you might have shared some intimate secrets and failings with your gaslighter in confidence. This would be used against you in snide remarks when fights occur.

- **They Are Obsessed With How You Look:** How you look is of utmost importance to them. This is not a loving gesture from them. Their concern is not to improve your image. It is part of their manipulative tactics. They want to control how you look, the outfits you choose, and so on.

- **They Are Very Jealous:** Gaslighters would never want you to be close to other friends, especially the male friends. They are very jealous and see everybody close to you as a threat. They will try to isolate you from everybody else. So, in order not to hurt their feelings, you're very careful around your male colleagues or acquaintances.

- **They Drain You Overtime:** Gaslighters will drain you over time. This they do gradually and in very subtle means, that you don't realize what's happening. At the beginning of the relationship, it's all lovey-dovey. He compliments you and all. Then comes the sudden outburst of criticisms. You're left confused. This is what he wants, as this confusion drains your psyche over a period of time.

- **They Project Their Emotion:** It's like a defence mechanism for them. They don't want to deal with their own feelings. They would rather project these feelings to you. It's a classic Freudian projection in play here. A gaslighter may be cheating on you, but would seriously accuse you of cheating on him.

- **They Don't Keep Promises:** A gaslighter would promise you heaven on earth, and intentionally break those promises. They make promises they don't intend keeping. To them, promises are made to be broken.

- **They Have Anger Issues:** They're not role-models when it comes to anger management. While they might hide these flaws at the beginning of the relationship, they will eventually slip and end up revealing their true selves. When angry they're susceptible to throwing tantrums and acting in ways you never thought possible.

- **They Never Admit To Mistakes:** Gaslighters love blaming others for their slip-ups. Everyone is the problem except them, of course. When confronted with this behaviour, they complain about being the subject of undue criticism. About being unfairly targeted. This is a sort of emotional blackmail for the victims. It can be tiring.

- **They Still Strike When You're Down And Out:** Not satisfied with the well-thought-out damage they've caused their victims, they still find ways to inflict more pains when their victims are already down and out. There's this sadistic pleasure they derive from knowing they're the source of your pain.

- **They Tell Mutual Friends About Your Failings:** Don't be surprised when mutual friends of yours start giving you side-eyes and uncomfortable glances when you're around. Your gaslighter may have been spreading untoward stories about you to them. Things you told him in confidence are repeated to friends. Your friends now start seeing you in a different light.

CHAPTER FOUR:

Ways Gaslighters Manipulate And Control Relationships

- **By Constantly Repeating Your Worst Fears:** Gaslighters are very good at using this tool to get at you. "You're fat", " I think you're just a failure", "You mean you failed your bar exams again? Maybe you're not just up to it. Please try something else". These are some examples of your fears your gaslighters may use against you, to ensure he has control over you. They are his secret weapons to keep you in check.

- **They Threaten To Leave You:** He knows you idolize him. He knows you've made him the centre of your world. This was his plan all along. To get you to that point where the mere thought of his abandoning the relationship makes you cringe in fear. So, to keep you within his control, he invokes these threats regularly - "no one will love you if I leave", "you will never find any fun guy like me". He's made you believe this, so you would do anything to make him stay and not leave.

- **Comparisons:** This is one of the gaslighter's major weapon. By citing the image of an ideal person out there he considers his standard, he's making you strive to meet those expectations. He knows you can't measure up to that standard. And try as hard as you may, he's always in the background sabotaging your efforts. This constant effort on your part to meet his ideal standard will make you want to stay in the relationship and prove your worth to him.

- **Incite Other Troubled Relationships You've Had:** When the both of you start having issues in your relationship, he will bring up other troubled relationships you've had in the past, or maybe having. "Maybe that's why your first boyfriend left you. You nag a lot", "maybe that's why your Dad threw you out. You're too stubborn". You would believe these cheap blackmails, and so strive harder to make your current relationship with him work out. After a history of troubled relationships in the past, you just want to break this stereotype.

- **They Make You Doubt Your Own Perceptions And Sense Of Reality:** With a gaslighter, you're always thinking - "am I really crazy?", "am I really delusional like he says I am?". Gaslighters would thoroughly distort your sense of perception. They will leave you constantly doubting yourself or sense of reality.

- **They Will Use Your Standards Against You:** They know what your ideals are, so they will use them against you. " I thought you hated impulse-buying?", "couples are supposed to take the fall for each other". You want to live up to your own standards, so you end up going along with their every prompting.

CHAPTER FIVE:

Why You Need To Stop Gaslighters

Recognizing gaslighting as the psychological abuse it is, will enable you shut it out once its signs begin to appear in a relationship. Being in a gaslighting relationship is unhealthy for you in every aspect - physically, psychologically, and emotionally. It messes up with your head and causes you to lose the very essence of yourself. You may need to stop that gaslighter for the following reasons:

- **They Mess Up Their Victim's Head:** Nothing can be more devastating than losing your very essence. Your unique being. Those particular traits that make you "you". And this is what gaslighters do. They mess up with their victim's head and have them questioning who they really are. This is one terrible situation nobody wants to find him or herself. Walking away early in the relationship, will break their effect on you. Do not try reasoning with them. Diplomacy is not one of their strong points.

- **Leave Their Victims With Guilt All Over:** Gaslighters employ the guilt-trip tactic. It is an emotional manipulative tactic they use on their victims. They make their victims feel trapped with guilt all over. They don't know where this feeling is coming from, this is because the gaslighter acts like he's the victim.

- **They Leave Their Victim In A State Of Shame:** After all the undeserved criticisms, then comes the feeling of shame. The victim is left to feel responsible for all the wrongs going on in the relationship. Definitely not a good place to be. He knows this feeling of shame would break down your self-confidence, so he goes ahead to gaslight you.

- **They Lower Your Self-Esteem And Self-Confidence:** Critical signs to look out for in victims of gaslighting abuse are the low self-esteem and a total loss of self-confidence. After being told several lies repeatedly by their gaslighters, the victim's self-esteem is severely eroded. They now believe they are simply not enough. The more you hang onto a gaslighter to regain your self-esteem, the more it's being nibbled at. The only way you can be helped is to break free from their grip by leaving the toxic environment.

- **Feelings Of Depression:** Victims of gaslighters are always depressed. This is caused by a nagging feeling of losing themselves overtime. They feel less happy. Sometimes, many good things might be happening to them all at once, yet they still feel less happy. They are yet to win the approval of someone they have come to loved, so they feel like failures.

- **Feelings of Hopelessness:** Victims of gaslighting abuse suffer from severe cases of hopelessness. There may be lots of good things going on their lives, yet, it doesn't help their cause one bit. There is also a certain numbness they feel towards everything that is happening around them.

- **Feelings of Anger:** They feel anger towards their gaslighters, friends and families alike. No one is spared their anger. They feel this anger towards their gaslighters because they are the reason for their abuse and to families and friends because they feel let down by them. A kind of abandonment.

- **Suicide:** Abuse in relationships is one of the causes of suicide. Being gaslighted leaves one with a feeling of despondency. For these people, they feel like life is no longer worth living, and there's no way out of their problems. Suicide seems the surest way out.

CHAPTER SIX:

How To Stop Gaslighting Abuse

In every gaslighting abuse, there is a silver lining. In such a relationship, it takes two to tango. The power your gaslighter holds over you, his victim, is only true up to the extent you allow him. While it is definitely not easy to just break off from the relationship, it is exactly what you need to do. Gaslighters are not your regular diplomats. That is to say, they're not reasonable. So stop trying to reason with them. Also, while it may seem like you do not have a choice to walk away, please know that you certainly do. They may have told you how no one will accept you, how they're simply putting up with you. This is nothing but a trick to keep you in the relationship and under their control. Know this - You can simply opt-out. And if you choose to stay and fight off their gaslighting behaviour, it should be done at your own terms.

Gaslighting abuse occurs because the victim wants to stay and get her gaslighter to see things from her own point of view. And why this desperate moves to win the gaslighter to her side? Because she awfully wants to win his approval. It is life support for them. His approval would make her feel whole once more. Getting this approval means she finally gets to make him accede to her own sense of reality. It is a victory for her if she achieves this feat. After a series of distortions to her truth, it confirms she wasn't crazy or delusional like he made her look. Know this - this will never happen. The gaslighting effect came through because he succeeded in eroding your sense of reality. He just can't soft-pedal. That means his grip over you would be broken. Which Magician knowingly allows the spell over his victim to be broken? His agreeing to your sense of perception breaks off the whole control plot and power play he's engaged in.

35

You don't need his approval to feel whole. You are enough just as you are. You surely don't need anybody's approval to be human.

Again, you must stop making excuses for your gaslighter and do not accept any from them either. Do not rationalize their failings. If they've failed to act, then they must accept the responsibility.

Furthermore, you will have to set limits on what's acceptable to you, and what's not. These limits should never be toyed with. It gives you a sense of what you're willing to put up with, and puts in perspective how your gaslighter regards you. If he crosses this red line numerous times, without the slightest care in the world, then opt-out of the whole affair.

You can trust your own sense of reality. When your gaslighter does not agree with your point of view, take it with a pinch of salt. Trust what you see and hear and don't allow your gaslighter's opinion overwhelm yours. When he sees you're not buying into his narratives anymore, he will begin to back-pedal. When this happens, he may leave the relationship on his own volition.

Finally, be honest with yourself. Access your relationship thoroughly to gauge what point it is right now. Do you need therapy? Is the abuse something you can handle on your own? Are you happy? Do you feel the need to put a stop to the way he constantly puts you down? Your answers to these and many more questions you will be raising is key to knowing the next steps to take. In all, never forget your one leverage - you can always walk away.

CHAPTER SEVEN:

Emotional Intelligence and How It Works Well in Dealing with Gaslighting Abuse

Emotional Intelligence - Daniel Goleman's 1995 bestseller, " Emotional Intelligence: Why It Matters More Than IQ" popularized this term and brought it into the mainstream. Though Goleman's treatise on emotional intelligence was focused on how it can drive leadership skills, it found useful applications in other areas such as Job performance, physical and mental health, self-esteem and drug addictions. Mental health is what we are concerned about. We would be looking at how emotional intelligence can help victims of gaslighting abuse deal with its after-effects.

What is Emotional Intelligence? Peter Salovey and John Mayer gave perhaps, one of the most accepted definitions of the term, defining it as "the ability to monitor one's own and other people's emotions, to discriminate between different emotions and label them appropriately, and to use emotional information to guide thinking and behaviour".

Keying into one's emotions is the basic theme of emotional intelligence and this is one ability that will help victims heal faster and face their gaslighters. It is no gainsaying the fact that emotions drive our relationships and he who has a grip on his emotions will form the best relationship with others. As Aristotle said "Man know thyself", you must know thyself before you can gain deep insights into others.

Studies have found out that women undergoing all forms of abuse generally have lower emotional intelligence. Their abilities and skills making up emotional intelligence are also less developed [Konstantinos, et al, 2016]. Therefore, finding ways to increase your emotional quotient will help you deal with gaslighting abuse. You can do so through the following ways:

- **Learning to respond to conflict situations instead of reacting to them:** The role of your gaslighter is to stir up conflict, situations that will draw up feelings of hatred and anger. These feelings will drain you constantly if you react to them rather than responding in a well-thought-out manner. Staying calm when your gaslighter would expect you to be worked-up, will give them the right signal that you can no longer be excited emotionally by their actions or lack of it. Gradually, their hold over you is broken.

- **Observe your own feelings:** Paying attention to how you're feeling throughout the day will give you a clue on how certain emotions are stirred up in you through stressful situations. It will also give you the ability to recognize and name your emotions - anger, self-pity, hatred, fear etc. When we recognize and tag our feelings, they tend to lose their destructive hold over us.

- **Communicate assertively**: When you communicate assertively you earn respect without coming across as aggressive or too passive. When you make your feelings known in an active manner, you gain respect. Your gaslighter will learn to take your feelings more serious.

- **Learn to question your own opinions:** Opinion is as cheap as it gets and everyone's entitled to it. We live in an opinionated world where people throw all kinds of opinions on our face. These opinions are likely to rub off on us over time. Therefore, learn to question every opinion, yours especially. To be sure they align with your core values and not just an opinion that has rubbed off on you unknowingly.

- **Take criticism well**: Veiled or direct criticism is also a tool for the gaslighter, to hit you where it hurts the most. When they throw such criticisms, don't get defensive. Instead, analyse the criticism, its source and understand where it's coming from. Though harsh, some criticisms can get us to improve ourselves and the overall quality of our lives. Take those ones that improve you well. Others that are meant to hurt you should be quietly waved off and given less thought to.

CHAPTER EIGHT:

Recovering From Gaslighting

Recovering from gaslighting is not as easy as everybody thinks. But it's much possible. Just like an addiction that we can break off with the right mindset and support, gaslighting abuse can be stopped also. With the right support system, you can recover from years of abuse and become the best version of yourself. Gaslighting abuse is a mental health problem. Years of abuse at the hands of your gaslighter might have messed up with your head and thought-patterns. So, considering therapy, is key to full recovery.

- **Identifying the problem:** It takes a lot of courage to admit that you're in a gaslighting relationship. It is usually an embarrassing situation. Nobody likes admitting to being taken for a ride, especially by people we have come to love and trust. It's hard being a tool for manipulation. It makes us think less of ourselves. Know you're not the problem. Your gaslighter is. Your gaslighting abuse might have been pointed out by concerned friends and family members, by a Mental Health Professional or even by your researching it yourself. Whichever way you found out about your ordeal, it's good the problem's been identified, because that is a major step towards recovery.

- **Taking to therapy:** Talking to a Mental Health Professional, especially one who is versed in the field of gaslighting really helps. Talking is a form of therapy. It releases the pent-up anger, resentment and hatred you may have towards yourself and your gaslighter. It's a form of catharsis. A therapist is able to break down these feelings for you, putting them in the right perspective. After years of brainwashing tactics by your gaslighter, you need someone who would be able to steer you back to the person you were before the series of abuse began.

Your therapist will be able to help you build a good concept of yourself once again. Your confidence is restored and your self-esteem is built up from scratch.

- **Give the relationship a break:** There's no way around it. Giving the relationship a break will help you heal properly. That's not to say you need to leave permanently. In a situation where you have a marital relationship with your gaslighter, leaving may actually be complicated. A period of separation is usually advised. There are cases where your gaslighter might not be aware of his gaslighting tendencies and how these tendencies are causing havoc to the relationship. With the right therapy, and motivation on his part, your gaslighter may find the help he needs. Whether you stay in the relationship or choose to opt-out, it's all up to you. But a serious path towards recovery means you two just have to stay apart for some time. This healing period will allow you regain the renewed ability to do things on your own without their pervasive influence. You've been at their mercy for a number of years. Now is the time to learn to do things without their help or opinions.

- **Give yourself a break:** After years of gaslighting abuse, you've come to believe a series of damning reports about yourself. Years of abuse have made you your own worst critic. After a while, you might even come to think of yourself as deserving of every treatment you got at the hands of your gaslighter. As you slowly recover, you need to break the cycle of these negative thinking. Stop blaming yourself for the actions of your gaslighter. Self-care is critical to your recovery program. Get enough sleep, eat well, engage in exercises and then meditate.

- **Empower yourself:** Gaslighting abuse can make you feel like the most incompetent person in the whole world who can't seem to do just about anything right. These feelings about yourself should be done away with. Begin by listing your strengths. Then move on to start doing things you feel competent at, no matter how mundane others may term them to be. Join a support group and surround yourself with people who recognize your strengths. Those with critical opinions about you should be avoided. They attract negative energy and drain your strength.

Follow these steps and you can become a beautiful version of yourself in no distant time.

CHAPTER NINE:

Self-consciousness - A Strategy For Dealing With Emotional Manipulators

The word "self-consciousness" has been taken to mean being uncomfortable with yourself and worried about disproval from other people. It is often taken as an exaggerated focus on ourselves and how others perceive us. When broken down into its initial psychological or philosophical meaning, it is not such a bad term, as it means a heightened sense of self-awareness. It is the capacity for introspection, the ability to look inward and determine our essence. With a heightened sense of self-awareness comes the ability to understand your own feelings, behaviours and motives. And a person who has achieved this high level of self-awareness or self-consciousness is no tool for emotional manipulators. They know you cannot be toyed with.

Self-consciousness is actually a part of your overall emotional intelligence strategy in dealing with manipulators. This strategy can start by learning how to recognize and label your emotions. When you are more aware of how you feel at every given point in time, nobody can throwback your emotions at you as a form of manipulation tactics. You may be at a low point in your life after going through a bitter divorce or breakup. Emotions like sadness, loneliness, anger, shock are stirred up during this period. This is a period when you are highly vulnerable to emotional manipulators. They might seem charming at first, saying and doing all the right things. All these actions are geared towards winning your heart. You're like a goal for them. Once you fall for their antics, you become a tool in their hands. They could then mould you to whatever they wanted. A heightened self-consciousness would reveal your own vulnerability to you before others pick up the scent. That way you can fight off their tactics.

Adopting self-consciousness strategy would also help identify your thoughts and what goes through your head. Self-defeating thoughts are identified and laid bare. Your self-critical monologues are also reviewed. Once noticed, steps are taken to rid these negative thoughts from your consciousness. Emotional manipulators possess traits such as the ability to "read" people which makes them dangerous. They can recognize your low self-esteem and use it to further run you down. It's a power play for them. They want control over you and the slightest hint they get about your vulnerability makes you an easy target for them.

Self-consciousness increases your intuition. We all possess this innate gut feeling. It gives us that sense that some things do not feel right during certain moments. A self-conscious person has this intuitive sense on a very high scale. Emotional manipulators can sense when people are onto them. Your intuitive level can serve as a red flag for them. That way they get to leave you alone and look for their next easy prey. Your high intuitive level would also serve as a guide to help you spot these manipulators. That way you will only accept direct responses from them, giving them no time to deflect issues. When you spot one, you're able to call them out and force them to accept responsibilities.

Self-consciousness is a strategy that works against manipulators. People who have spouses who are emotionally manipulative should apply this strategy often. It keeps their head above water and ensures they are not overwhelmed by the herald of issues that are likely to crop up in a relationship.

CHAPTER TEN:

Dealing With A Narcissistic Partner

Narcissism is a disorder in which a person has an inflated sense of self-importance. It describes an excessive interest, admiration or absorption in one's self and one's physical appearance. It is actually a personality disorder which was only recently added to the Diagnostic and Statistics Manual (DSM), in 1980. Though it can be present in both genders, it is more prevalent in males, with the lastest DSM study indicating that as much as seventy-five per cent of narcissists are men.

Being in a relationship with a narcissistic partner is draining, to say the least. They would overwhelm you in every respect and can cause you to repeatedly doubt yourself. Victims who have survived a narcissistic partner or currently in a relationship with one are usually dazed and confused.

Narcissistics are usually the perfect partners in the initial stages of a relationship. They make you feel loved and appreciated. They exhibit the best of qualities and make all the right feelings come alive in you. This usually, is the first plot in a story that's about to turn sour. As the relationship progresses, then comes the sudden mean remarks, outright criticisms and subtle put-downs. Don't be confused at this point, though most victims usually are. The fact of the matter is that you were not loved by him, to begin with. He merely used you as a source of his narcissistic supply, a word which describes anybody the narcissistic uses to promote his false sense of superiority. He needs people to achieve this. As long as you are the steady source of his supply, he is draped in his cloak of pseudo-love. That describes the feeling of love you felt from him initially. Once you withdraw this supply, maybe through acts that deflate his sense of entitlement - criticisms, challenging his self-worth, you would definitely be discarded like a bad habit. That is why narcissists are in constant search for new partners, to commence the cycle all over again. Admiration, constant attention and hero-worship from others are like a drug for them. The following strategies can help you deal with a narcissistic partner.

1. **Narcissistic do not understand they are Narcissist:** It has been said that there is no cure for this disorder, that it can only be managed. One of the reasons for such postulations is that narcissists do not understand they are narcissists. They don't see themselves how others see them, and so are less likely to seek help or go for therapy. However, recent research shows that narcissists are very much aware of who they are and how people perceive them. The next question that follows is - then why keep up with this destructive personality if they are very much aware? Two answers were proffered

for this question. Firstly, narcissists believe people are yet to see how awesome they are. Maybe when they do, they would recognize their brilliance and give them their due credits. Secondly, narcissists believe people are jealous of them. They receive negative feedbacks of people with a pinch of salt, tagging these responses as feedbacks of people who covet their exceptional gifts. Understanding this concept as the partner would make you seek professional help for them or adapt to their traits.

2. **They won't change:** Narcissism is one trait which has its root causes linked to different sources - environment (a situation where parents excessively adore or criticize the child), Genetics (inherited characteristics), and Neurobiology (the connection between the brain and behaviour). It's a complex

disorder, so it's unlikely the person would change. It's a personality trait that has a long-standing history in the individual concerned. So stop trying to change them. Seeing them for who they really are one of the steps in dealing with them. Your moves to change them may be met with resistance. Therefore, there's nothing much you can do to change them.

3. **Remove the cloak of Denial:** It was easy to be charmed by their seemingly high level of confidence and self-esteem. They presented a perfect picture of themselves and so, you were swayed. You refuse to believe they are narcissistics. You keep on making excuses for them, blaming their cruel attitudes on stress and pressure from work. The earlier you accept their behaviour for what it is, the better for you in setting clear boundaries. By acceptance, you're

ready to choose between leaving and staying. If you're staying, then on what terms.

4. **Understand you played no part in their behaviour:** Do not get caught up in the "it's all my fault" thinking. Never you come to think of yourself as playing a role in the abusive treatments meted out to you. Initially, you were shown love, appreciation, and he adored you in every aspect. Then came the part where he suddenly withdrew all forms of affections. You will definitely start thinking you did something wrong to cause this sudden switch in his behaviour. You did not. It was all part of the end-game. Now, he's played it to the fullest. Understand this and save yourself the stress.

5. **Detach with love:** Once you've come to terms with his behaviour, begin the process of detaching with love. This means basically shutting out the

person's behaviour, while still keeping the love you have for him. You very much still care for him, but you will no longer accept the blame he heaps on you. You now deflect them, knowing it's the disorder in him acting up.

At the centre of the aforementioned coping strategies is the key message - take care of yourself. Your narcissistic partner is too self-absorbed to do that for you. He is too caught up in his own little world to care about your feelings and emotions. So, whether you choose to stay or not, your interest is paramount and should take centre-stage.

CHAPTER ELEVEN:

Dealing With Emotional Abusers And Gaslighters At Work

It is true that gaslighting abuse extends beyond romantic relationships into the workplace. In the professional setting, gaslighters would do anything, including using underarm and manipulative tactics to wreck your professional life. They will go out of their way to sabotage your career prospects while praising you in front of everyone. They're good at complimenting you when you're around, but say bad things behind your back to your superiors and those that matter in your workplace. They're also subtle in the way they go about their activities, so as not arouse suspicions.

How To Know You're Dealing With A Gaslighter At Your Workplace

- They take credits for your efforts.

- They tell your supervisors and superiors that you're incompetent. They may go extra lengths to prove these assertions.
- They give glowing remarks about you in front of your colleagues but spread negative rumours about you. This is done in the most subtle way possible.
- They sabotage your efforts.
- They may sexually harass you.
- They try to take the shine in every group project.
- They try to prevent you from attending major and important meetings by not informing you about such meetings or giving you the wrong timing.
- They may try to incite you to do something that's unethical, so as to blackmail you with it in the nearest future.

Gaslighters are nightmares to work with, and as time goes on, you will start approaching your workplace with fear and resentments, thinking everybody is out to get you. Having a gaslighter as your direct boss is the most insidious of all. He may feel you're out to get his job, and so commence a campaign of underarm tactics against you. He gives you bad reviews during appraisals, even when the facts point to an excellent job performance by you, he gives you complex projects with deadlines that are difficult to meet and generally makes your life a living hell in the office.

How To Cope With Them

- Document every project you undertake, so they don't get undeserved credits for your efforts.
- If you gaslighter is your direct boss, file for transfer to a different department. If this is not possible, work with them from a distance and avoid much contact with them. All meetings should be in an open place.
- Demand a CCTV camera be installed in your office. Gaslighters can plant

illegal materials in your office to set you up.

- Ensure you do not have a public spat with your gaslighter. They may turn the tide against you. Moreover, gaslighters enjoy this sort of public confrontations. Employ subtle approaches instead.
- Record every encounter during group projects.

If the situation does not improve with time, you may have to resign and seek employment elsewhere. Do not take your resignation as a victory for you gaslighter. Take it as a chance to leave a toxic environment.

CHAPTER THIRTEEN:

How To Talk So People Can Listen

Influencing people through your speeches, group discussions, project meetings, or even private encounters is critical to your success in every area of your life. The world has been blessed with great orators who have changed the world with moving speeches. They have moved men to act with highly emotional and thought-provoking speeches. Men such as Martin Luther King, Barack Obama, Steve Jobs, Abraham Lincoln Winston Churchill, Mahatma Gandhi, and lots more, have moved nations to act through endearing speeches. These men remain people of influence, long after they have left the stage because they got people to listen. You can achieve the same feat today by applying these steps:

1. **Raise Your Confidence Level:** If you are actually going to say something, then

do so with confidence. Nothing inspires crazy followership than a leader who's confident of what he is really saying. Do you believe what you are going to say is important? Then say it with confidence. Eliminate your fears and doubts. These are your greatest impediments to thought-provoking speeches. Once overcome, there's no limit to the crowd you can move by your speeches. Confidence is really a body language. And your audience can spot it. They see through you. Since body language is said to account for about 55 per cent of the message a speaker is trying to pass across, maybe you should possess more of it. [Albert Mehrabian, UCLA].

2. **Eye Contact:** Eye contact is a human connection. In an age where Artificial Intelligence, chatbots, and speech software solutions are taking over the communication gap, this connection is highly sought after for interpersonal communication. If you can't connect

with your audience through eye contact, then you might as well employ a robot to pass your message across. Maintain eye contact with your audience. It engages them and makes them a part of any narrative, movement, or ideology you might be projecting.

3. **Voice Tone And Volume:** The expression, "it is not what you say, but how you say it" comes readily to mind. Mehrabian also stated that 38 per cent of a speaker's message was contained in his voice tone. Your vocal tone will invariably influence your confidence level. They both work hand-in-hand. By changing the tone of your voice, it affects the influence of your message on your audience.

4. **Adjust To Your Audience Style:** Toreja Curic of Page Group is noted for his four main styles of communication. They are the Drivers, the Analytical, the Expressive and the Amiable. Your audience will only relate with the style

they identify most with. As a speaker, it is your job to learn all styles, so you can use them to your advantage. When speaking quickly review all styles and notice which of them arouses your audience, then stick with that. Though your audience might be mixed with people with varying styles, cater to the needs of the majority.

5. **Create Twitter-like Headlines:** This was the aspect of presentation where Steve Jobs walked like a colossus. He made short witty headlines that stood out and created huge impressions in the minds of his audience.

6. **Get To The Heart Of The Matter:** Herein you must answer the question that matters most to your audience. What are your listeners interested in? Why should they listen to you? Answer these questions beforehand and you're sure to have an audience who would kill off every distraction to hear you out.

CHAPTER FOURTEEN:

How To Rebuild Yourself Emotionally

Surviving an abusive relationship, be it with a narcissistic partner, a gaslighting parent or a boyfriend who is physically abusive, leaves you an emotional wreck. You generally lose touch with yourself, becoming less and less unsure of yourself and your emotions. It takes a lot of work rebuilding yourself and getting your emotions back in check. The following steps can get you back on track on the road to becoming emotionally strong once again.

- **Own Your Past:** Owning your past means being thankful for them no matter your struggles with abuse. Throw away the self-defeating thoughts that are sure to creep in once in a while. Your past struggles are currently making you the renewed and beautiful soul you're turning out to be. The mistakes are lessons to use as guides to your mentees. Therefore, honour these struggles and wear them as a badge of honour. They're reminders of where you've been and how far you've come.

- **Find A Support Group:** Spending quality time with people of like minds who have undergone the same struggles as you have, can be soul-lifting. These are people who understand you and can truly listen when you tell your stories. They can serve as motivations to be a better version of yourself. It's not always an easy process, that is, the path to recovery, but this group are always there to support you in the event of your relapse.

- **Practise Mindfulness:** By practising mindfulness, you're creating quality time for yourself to think, breath, be quiet and just observe your feelings. This can be done at any time or place - at the office, at home, while shopping, at the park. All you need is a space to yourself to enable you connect with your senses.

- **Express Your Emotions:** There are days when you would feel like crying as you reminisce about past struggles. You may feel sad, angry at the world, at yourself and just about anyone, especially, your abuser. Feel free, express your emotions. These emotions are cathartic in themselves and should be embraced for what they are.

- **Never Judge Yourself:** When the inner self-critical monologue begins to surface, it should be shut down immediately. While you can be open to constructive self-criticisms, as these can lead to self-improvement over time, negative self-talk should be avoided. They can become a vicious cycle which will be difficult to break through from.

- **Find Love Once More:** You're welcome to take emotional risks such as finding love once more or allowing it find you. Either way, do not reject people who truly care and may want to be part of your rebuilding process. It's okay to be vulnerabe. Brené Brown in her powerful Tedtalk, "The power of vulnerability" said, "Vulnerability is the core, the heat, the centre of meaningful human experience". That feeling to want to shut down your heart, to prevent further heartbreaks is vulnerability and it is a normal feeling afterall. So, dare once more. Dare greatly.

CHAPTER FIFTEEN:

How to Stop Sociopaths

Sociopaths are in the long line of manipulative personalities who employ charming tactics to get to their victims. Lack of empathy is one of their major traits, and constantly using people to achieve their gains, is one of the things they're known for. It's important to always be a step ahead of the sociopath. Employing your A-game when dealing with them is one of the effective ways to handle them. You can employ these tactics:

1. Recognize that they can be charming. That's one of the ways they get you to lower your guard. Don't be charmed by their disposition. If you find a person, especially one you suspect to be a sociopath, to be unusually charming and trying to gain your attention, increase you alertness and stay self-aware.

2. They are expert manipulators. When a sociopath approaches you with any form of proposal, do not take what they say and do at face value. Dig deeper to enable you see through their schemes.

3. You might consider limiting interactions with them. Every encounter with them can leave you emotionally drained. Therefore, limit contact to as much as possible.

4. Do not reveal intimate details about yourself. Keep things on a neutral level. Your personal failings, fears weakpoints are secrets about you that a sociopath should never get hold of. They can use these informations to hurt you deeply.

5. Do not reveal what makes you happy or sad. This information can be used to trigger your emotional soft spots.

6. Keep your plans close to your chest. Never disclose them to a sociopath.

With a sociopath, anything is possible. Always stay a step ahead of them.

CHAPTER SEVENTEEN:

Dealing with Denial

In relationships, many problems are sure to spring up. One of such problems is the relationship itself coming to an end. Some people are usually prepared for this, and so, achieve closure in record time. Some are usually ill-prepared and it hits them in the face like a huge wave. For these ones, they can't believe it's really over. They are more likely to distort facts to fit in with their own reality. Denial is like a coping mechanism and they have it in full doses. Denial is also like a form of prison, and you can't really see the light if you're right in it. Moving on is your best bet.

No one said it would be easy. Ending a relationship with someone who has brought you joy in the past, someone with whom you've shared intimate secrets and your deepest fears with, is hard and painful, to put it mildly. But also painful is the emotional black hole you put yourself in, when you decide to live in denial of your problems.

Denial does not only happen in romantic relationships. It does happen in other relationships too - familial, professional and business relationships. A parent who is yet to acknowledge her son's addiction is living in denial. The Employer who is yet to believe his most trusted and loyal employee has been embezzling the company's funds for years now, is living in denial. Denial helps us escape our fears and tough reality. No wonder many embrace it. It's their safe zone.

Staying in the safe zone of denial won't solve your problems. Accepting reality and facing your problems squarely, is what gives you that giant leap you need. You can start with baby steps though. By simply acknowledging the reality staring you right in the face, you're on your way to moving past your denials! To recover fully from denial, take these steps:

1. **Look for Signs of Denials:** Most people in a state of denial won't readily admit. The following can give you a clue - are you making excuses? Are you rationalizing the problem? Are you looking for closure before you move on? Closure in the form of expecting a call from your ex giving you a sort of relationship postmortem. These are blockages to deny the truth of our experience and should be done with.

2. **Get A Neutral Feedback:** This can serve as a dose of reality check. Getting the feedback of a neutral party, to tell you as it is, can help you break the chains of denial.

3. **Acknowledge Your Reality:** By accepting what we cannot change, to borrow from our "serenity prayer" helps us move in the right direction and give up our denial.

4. **Seek Professional Help:** Talking to someone, especially a therapist, can help.

They're able to put your emotions in the right perspective for you.

Anyone can succumb to the alluring grip of denial. No one is immune. Breaking up with a love interest, erasing memorable experiences with them, moving on and just acting like nothing happened is a process fit for psychopaths and not normal humans with emotions. We all must experience one or two painful events that would seem impossible to let go. This is normal. Denial can be a temporal state we use to manage our tough reality. But when it begins to tamper with our forging ahead, it should be snapped out from and discarded with.

Other Books by The Same Author

- <u>How to Deal with Gaslighting: Recognize and Stop Hidden Psychological Manipulations and Abuse</u>

- <u>How to Deal with Emotional Immaturity: Cope with Emotionally Immature People in A Relationship, Work and Social Life</u>

- <u>How to Deal with Negative People: Protect Your Boundaries, Build Confidence, And Gain Respect</u>

- <u>Change Your Life:</u> **How to Overcome Anxiety, Depression and Negative Thinking**

- **<u>Anxiety and Phobia Workbook</u>: How to Overcome Anxiety and Panic Attacks**

- **<u>How to Deal with Difficult People</u>: Control the Situation! Overcome Your Annoying and Frustrating Coworkers, Friends, Parents, or Classmates**